SAVE THE TIGER

Sarah Eason

PowerKiDS press.

New York

Published in 2009 by The Rosen Publishing Group, Inc.
29 East 21st Street, New York, NY 10010

Illustrators: Andrew Geeson and Marijke Van Veldhoven
Designer: Paul Myerscough
Consultant: Michael Scott
U.S. Editor: Kara Murray

Photo Credits: Ardea/John Daniels front cover; Dreamstime p.8, p.16, p.18, p.26; FLPA/Gerard Lacz p.11 /Jurgen & Christine Sohns p.19 /Terry Whittaker p.23; Inmagine p.7; istockphoto p.4, p.5, p.10, p.14, p.21, p.28, poster; Photos.com p.9, p.15; Shutterstock p.6, p.12, p.13, p.17, p.20, p.22, p.24, p.25, p.27, p.29.

Library of Congress Cataloging-in-Publication Data

Eason, Sarah.
  Save the tiger / Sarah Eason. — 1st ed.
      p. cm. — (Save the)
  Includes index.
  ISBN 978-1-4358-2813-1 (library binding)
  1. Tigers—Juvenile literature. I. Title.
  QL737.C23E15 2009
  599.756—dc22

                            2008031800

Printed in China

Contents

Why Are Tigers So Special?

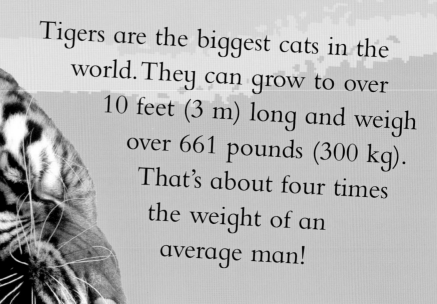

Tigers are the biggest cats in the world. They can grow to over 10 feet (3 m) long and weigh over 661 pounds (300 kg). That's about four times the weight of an average man!

grrrr

SAVE THE TIGER!

There are many things that you can do to help save the tiger. Look out for the Save the Tiger boxes in this book for ways in which you and your friends can help.

Tigers are incredibly powerful killers. Each tiger has soft pads beneath its feet, which help it quietly creep up on animals. Long curved claws are used to grab its **prey.** Tigers mainly hunt deer, buffalo and wild pigs. They have been known to kill and eat prey as large as leopards and pythons!

I am a magnificent swimmer. I can cross very wide rivers in search of new places to hunt.

My jaws are filled with 30 daggerlike, razor-sharp teeth.

Did You Know?

My pelt can have over 100 stripes!

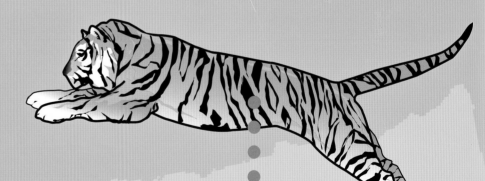

I can leap over 33 feet (10 m) in just one jump – that's the length of six fully grown men lying head to toe!

Why Is the Tiger in Danger?

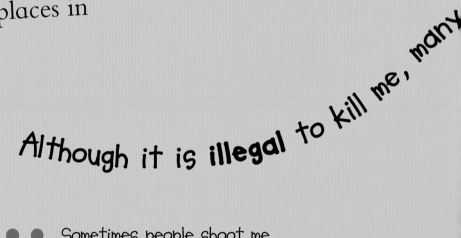

Did You Know?

I once lived in many parts of the world, from Turkey to all across south and east Asia.

One hundred years ago, at least 100,000 tigers lived in the wild. Today just 2,500 adult tigers roam free. Tigers are still hunted for their fur and bones. Much of the forest they live in has been destroyed by farming or building. There are now very few places in the world in which tigers can live.

Although it is illegal to kill me, many

Sometimes people shoot me and make my fur into a rug. My bones, fur, tail and other parts of my body are also made into medicines and sold in China and other parts of Asia.

Javan, Caspian and Bali tigers have not been seen in their home forests for 40 years. These tigers are probably now **extinct**.

Bali tiger

Javan tiger

Caspian tiger

poachers still hunt me.

SAVE THE TIGER!

Visit the World Wildlife Fund's Web site and discover how you can adopt a tiger: www.wwf.org

Where Do Tigers Live?

Tigers live in several different countries. Tigers live in big forests, where each tiger can have plenty of space and can hunt the animals that they eat. They hide behind grass and forest plants so they can creep up on their prey.

Did You Know?

Four out of every ten tiger forest areas have been destroyed.

There are now fewer places where tigers can live, because people have cut down large areas of forests to build towns and farms in their place.

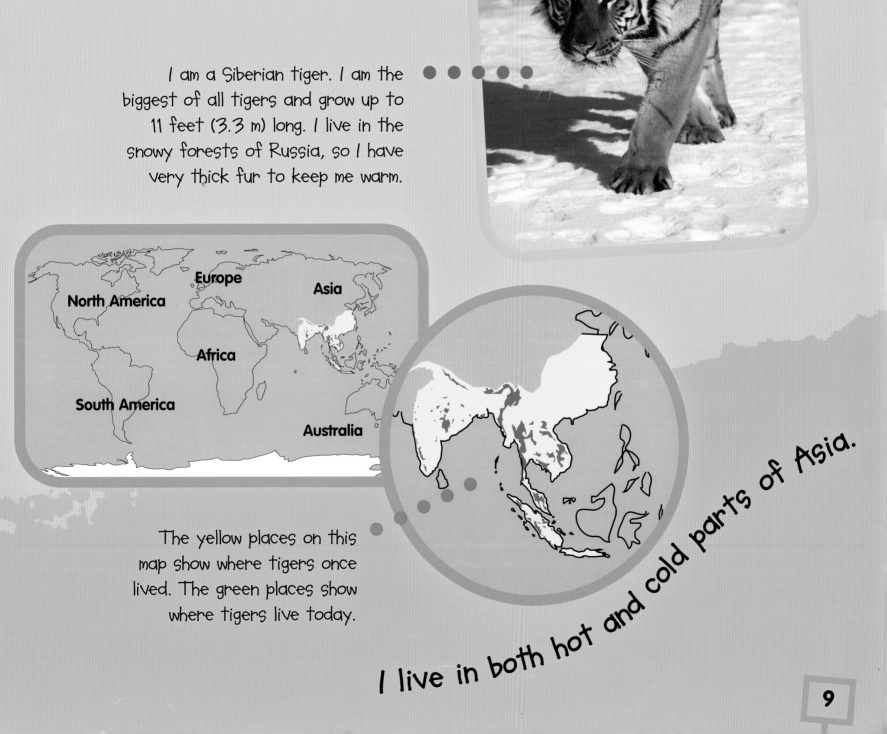

I am a Siberian tiger. I am the biggest of all tigers and grow up to 11 feet (3.3 m) long. I live in the snowy forests of Russia, so I have very thick fur to keep me warm.

North America

Europe

Asia

Africa

South America

Australia

The yellow places on this map show where tigers once lived. The green places show where tigers live today.

I live in both hot and cold parts of Asia.

Are All Tigers the Same?

There are five types of tiger still alive: the Siberian tiger (or Amur tiger), the South China tiger, the Indochinese tiger, the Sumatran tiger and the Bengal tiger. All of these tigers are in danger of becoming extinct unless more is done to protect them.

● ● ● ● ● ● ● I am a Sumatran tiger. I measure just 7 to 8 feet (2–2.5 m) long and I am the smallest of all tigers. Today, only 250 adult Sumatran tigers live in the Sumatran forest.

Only 50 South China tigers

striped fur

All tigers have these features in common.

long tail

strong jaw

powerful legs

SAVE THE TIGER!

Never buy anything that has been made from tigers. Some folk medicines and objects are made of tiger parts.

still live in the wild.

A few Bengal tigers, like myself, have almost white fur with brown stripes and blue eyes. No more than 2,000 Bengal tigers live in the wild, but we are still under threat from poachers.

11

How Do Tigers Make a Home?

Tigers like to live alone. They usually fight other tigers that stray onto their **territory**. Tigers need a very large territory so that they have plenty of animals to hunt for food.

I make a hiding place called a **den**, where I look after my babies. My den is usually made in a cave or a clump of long grass.

This tiger has wandered into my territory. I am fighting her to let her know that this is my home.

Tigers mark the edges of their territory by leaving scratch marks on trees. They also leave **scent markings** all over their territory. They do this by rubbing their faces against trees and by leaving urine and droppings where other tigers will smell them. This is a smelly message that tells other tigers to keep out!

I take a nap in the shade of long grass when it is hot.

SAVE THE TIGER!

Many rainforests in which tigers live are being destroyed. Never buy anything made with wood that might have come from rainforests.

13

What Do Tigers Eat?

Tigers are carnivores. That means they only eat meat. They will eat almost any animal they can catch. Their favorite foods are deer, goat, wild boar, water buffalo and cattle.

When I have

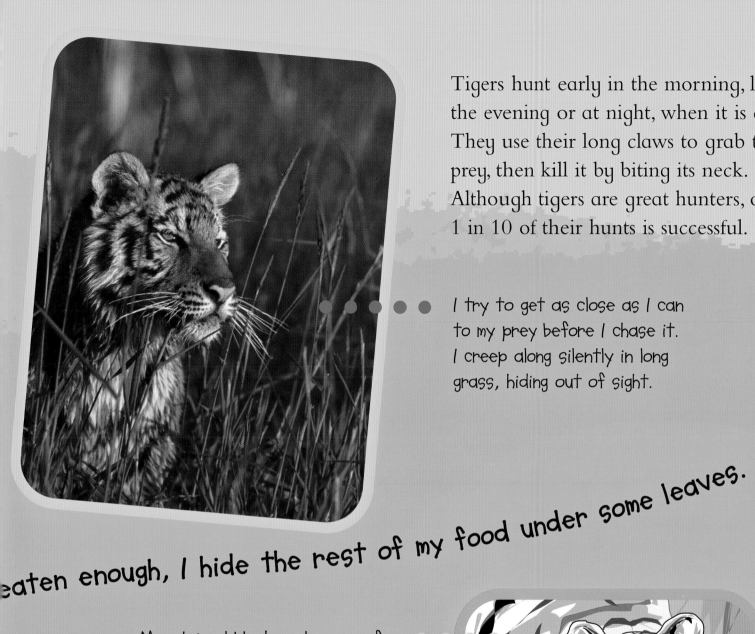

Tigers hunt early in the morning, late in the evening or at night, when it is cooler. They use their long claws to grab their prey, then kill it by biting its neck. Although tigers are great hunters, only 1 in 10 of their hunts is successful.

I try to get as close as I can to my prey before I chase it. I creep along silently in long grass, hiding out of sight.

eaten enough, I hide the rest of my food under some leaves.

My striped black and orange fur makes it difficult for other animals to see me hiding in the long grass and forest plants. This helps me creep up on them.

What Do Tigers Do All Day?

Tigers spend most of their day sleeping and most of their night hunting. When they are not sleeping or hunting, they roam around their territory to protect it from other tigers.

Did You Know?

Most cats hate water – but tigers love it!

splash, splash

Tigers love to cool down on hot days by lazing around the edge of a river or lake. Many animals come to the river to drink, so riverbanks make the perfect place for tigers to look out for dinner!

We like to keep ourselves clean by licking our fur with our rough tongues. We spend a lot of time **grooming** – just like house cats.

SAVE THE TIGER!

Teach your friends all about tigers. Why not ask your teacher if you can make a poster about tigers to put on a wall in your classroom?

I like to take a nap during the day.

How do Tigers Talk?

Tigers talk to each other in many different ways. They make lots of sounds and movements to let each other know how they feel. Each tiger's scent markings also send messages to other tigers.

roar, roar

I half-close my

Tigers show their feelings by roaring, hissing, purring and growling. Each sound has a different meaning. Tigers growl to show that they are angry and roar to let other tigers know where they are. A tiger's roar can be heard more than 2 miles (3 km) away.

I leave scratch markings on trees to show other tigers that this is my territory.

eyes when I am happy and sleepy.

When I am angry, I flatten my ears and show my teeth. That tells other tigers to stay out of my way.

Did you know?

Just like house cats, tigers twitch their tails to show that they are angry.

19

How Do Tigers Find a Mate?

Adult tigers live alone, so when they want to have babies, they must find a **mate**. Once a male and female have **mated**, the male tiger leaves. When the babies are born, the female cares for them by herself. A tiger's babies are called cubs.

Sniff, Sniff

SAVE THE TIGER!

Good zoos breed **tigers** that are in danger of becoming extinct. If you visit these zoos, the money you spend will help care for tigers there.

We are a male and female tiger. When we find each other, we rub our faces together and roll around. We stay together and play for a few days.

I give birth to my cubs 100 days after mating.

When a female tiger is ready to have cubs, she leaves special scent messages all over her territory. When a male tiger smells her scent, he understands that she is looking for a mate and he comes to find her.

When the nearest male tiger is very far away, I help him find me by roaring loudly.

How Do Tigers Raise Their Babies?

Mother tigers care for their cubs in a den. Tigers use a den only when they have young cubs. Tigers usually have between two and three cubs. The group of cubs is called a litter.

I practice hunting by pouncing on

SAVE THE TIGER!

When a tiger's mother is killed by poachers, it becomes an orphan. You can help tiger cubs by donating money to a tiger orphanage, where baby tigers are cared for.

Tiger cubs stay hidden in the safety of a den until they are old enough to hunt with their mother. A mother tiger feeds her babies with milk from her teats. When they are two months old, she starts to bring them meat.

I am only the size of a house cat when I am born. I need my mother to care for me until I am two years old.

the white tip at the end of my mother's tail.

My mother carries me by the loose skin around my neck. It may look painful, but it doesn't hurt.

Did You Know?

All baby tigers have blue eyes when they are born.

How Do Tigers Use Their Senses?

Tigers are much more sensitive to sights, sounds, smells, tastes and touch than humans. Because tigers are active at night, they use their excellent hearing and very sharp eyesight to find their prey in the dark.

I can see in the dark

I can recognize many different smells by curling back my lips and "tasting" the air.

Did You Know?

A tiger's eyes glow in the light of a torch or moonlight.

A tiger's large ears hear the tiniest rustle in the forest and help tigers find prey in the dark. As well as having excellent eyesight, tigers have sensitive whiskers that help them feel their way through bushes and rocks in the dark without scratching their faces.

My **pupils** grow very big in the dark to let more light into my eyes. This helps me see at night.

Six times better than a person!

SAVE THE TIGER!

Wildlife organizations **need money to care for tigers.** You could ask your teacher if your class or school could raise money to help save tigers.

Can Tigers and People Live Together?

Every year, more and more people are born. As the number of people in the world grows, more towns in which they can live are built on land that was once roamed by animals. This means that there is less and less space in which wild animals can live.

SAVE THE TIGER!

Tigers roam safely in game reserves. If you visit a tiger game reserve, all the money that you spend will help local people run the reserve and help keep tigers alive.

The largest Bengal tiger population is found in the Sundarbans forest, in India. The tigers in the forest are especially dangerous, up to 15 people have been killed there by tigers in recent years.

Wildlife organizations protect tiger **habitats**. Guards patrol the area to protect tigers from poachers so that they can live there safely.

I eat farm animals only when there are no wild animals to eat.

Did You Know?

Every year, more than 400 tigers are killed.

When people burn forests and grasslands to make space for farms or houses, many animals are killed and their homes are destroyed.

What Else Can You Do to Help Tigers?

Many people in the world are working very hard to save tigers. There are lots of things that you and your friends can do to help, too.

SAVE THE TIGER!

People are so poor in some countries that they kill and sell tigers. By buying Fair Trade goods you can help stop poverty and help the tiger.

Find out more about how you can help save tigers and their habitats by visiting this Web site: www.powerkidslinks.com/savethe/tiger/

Never buy anything that has been made from a tiger. Some jewelry is made from tiger body parts, such as this necklace, which is made from tiger teeth.

Why not adopt a tiger for a friend?

Our mother has been killed by poachers. We will live in an orphanage until we are old enough to return to the wild.

Glossary

breed (BREED) When animals give birth to young.

den (DEN) A home or hiding place of a wild animal.

extinct (ek-STINKT) When all of a type of animal or plant has died out forever.

game reserves (GAYM rih-ZURVZ) Protected places where animals can live safely in their natural habitat.

grooming (GROOM-ing) Cleaning the fur to remove dirt and insects.

habitats (HA-beh-tats) Where an animal or plant lives in the wild.

illegal (ih-LEE-gul) Against the law.

mate (MAYT) One of a pair of animals that make babies together.

mated (MAYT-ed) When a male and female animal make babies.

orphanage (OR-fuh-nij) A place for baby animals whose parents have died.

poachers (POH-cherz) People who kill or catch animals illegally.

poverty (PAH-ver-tee) When people find it difficult to live because they are so poor.

prey (PRAY) An animal that is hunted for food.

pupils (PYOO-pulz) Dark parts in the center of eyes.

scent markings (SENT MAHR-kingz) Special smells left by an animal.

territory (TER-uh-tor-ee) An area defended by an animal against others of its kind.

wildlife organizations (WYLD-lyf or-guh-nuh-ZAY-shunz) Groups that help and protect wild animals.

Index